EDINBURGH

Edited By Allie Jones

First published in Great Britain in 2017 by:

Young Writers
Remus House
Coltsfoot Drive
Peterborough
PE2 9BF
Telephone: 01733 890066
Website: www.youngwriters.co.uk

All Rights Reserved
Book Design by Spencer Hart
© Copyright Contributors 2017
SB ISBN 978-1-78820-239-8
Printed and bound in the UK by BookPrintingUK
Website: www.bookprintinguk.com
YB0321Z

FOREWORD

Welcome Reader!

Are you ready to discover weird and wonderful creatures that you'd never even dreamed of?

For Young Writers' latest competition we asked primary school pupils nationwide to create a creature of their own invention, and then write a story about it using just 100 words – a hard task indeed! However, they rose to the challenge magnificently and the result is this fantastic collection full of battling aliens, lonely creatures and mischievous monsters causing havoc!

Here at Young Writers our aim is to encourage creativity in children and to inspire a love of the written word, so it's great to get such an amazing response, with some absolutely fantastic stories.

Not only have these young authors created imaginative and inventive creatures, they've also crafted wonderful tales to showcase their creations. These stories are brimming with inspiration and cover a wide range of themes and emotions - from fun to fear and back again!

I'd like to congratulate all the young authors in 'Crazy Creatures - Edinburgh' - I hope this inspires them to continue with their creative writing.

Allie Jones

CONTENTS

Bonaly Primary School

Leen Nashed (9)	1
Isobel Morrice (9)	2
Erica Louise Sibley (9)	3
Calum Dall (9)	4
Kaylie Coleman (9)	5
Eilidh Chisholm (9)	6
Rachel Rose (9)	7
Rosie Forster (9)	8
Lucy Meiklejohn (9)	9
Daniel William Leslie (9)	10
Ben Sharman (9)	11
James Allen (10)	12
Jack Cook (10)	13
Emily McGillivray (9)	14
Zohaib Jafar (9)	15
Lauren E Rhynas (9)	16
Alexander Dey (10)	17
Kirsty Elizabeth Arnot (9)	18
Angus Hunter (10)	19
Nell Hauxwell-Douglas (9)	20
Joseph Cebula (9)	21
Aidan Hughes (10)	22
Alexander Stott (10)	23
Leo Edge (9)	24
Johny Pleki (9)	25
Anna Quin (9)	26
Kealan O'Shea-Morrans (9)	27
Anna Edwards (9)	28
Jemima Macaulay (9)	29
James Stark Millar (9)	30
Orlagh Belle Kennedy-Darke (9)	31
Magnus Johnston (10)	32
Daniel Haxton-Locke (9)	33

Bruntsfield Primary School

Evie Montgomery (9)	34
Eilidh Broster (9)	35
Bailey Geddes (10)	36
Mae Bailey (9)	37
Katie Tennet (10)	38
Erin Mahal (9)	39
Edward Roberts (9)	40
Robyn Sarah Lane (10)	41
Tilly Jo Harkes (10)	42
Camille Renwick Wilson (9)	43
Ida Mackay (9)	44
Amelia Page (9)	45
Teema Siddiki (9)	46
Ailsa McGregor (9)	47
JJ Liggins (9)	48
Ritika Sharma (9)	49
Eva Jourdan (9)	50
Elwyn Ichikawa-Bryant (9)	51
Elektra Skye Robertson (9)	52
Sophie McIntosh Burrows (9)	53
Joe Jannetta (9)	54
Eva Xin-Xin Stickland (9)	55
Natalie Lesniowolska (9)	56
Leo Cassidy (9)	57
Iona Ward (10)	58
Amber Hutton (9)	59
Percy Sutherland (9)	60
Marta Della Sala (9)	61
Connor MacKenzie (9)	62
Max Milne (9)	63
Sam Beattie (9)	64
Alex Thomson (10)	65
Athena Xantho Sintoris (9)	66
Max Johnston (9)	67

Muhammad Kashif (10)	68
Sophie Adams (9)	69
Finlay Lawson (10)	70
Ava McComb (10)	71
Saba Rashad (9)	72
Zara Rahman (10)	73
Rosie Kate Zisman (10)	74
Aisling Tierney (9)	75
Millie Orr (9)	76
Brodie Lindsay (10)	104
Ralph William Kelly (9)	105
Ioannis Tsirikos (10)	106
Lily Phanos (9)	107
Alexander Millar (10)	108
Arianna Coli (9)	109
Zac Lawson (10)	110

George Watson's College Junior School

Jess Mitchell (8)	77
Sarah Kerr (8)	78
Oliver Bond (8)	79
Noah Lucatelli (9)	80
Lucy Dunbar (8)	81
Louis Ferguson (8)	82
Aditi Patwari (8)	83
Stephen Carlos O'Neill (9)	84
Finlay Joseph Riley-McLean (9)	85
Jawan Fayez Fagiha (9)	86
Jasmine Mitchell (8)	87
Enam Evong (8)	88
Aaron Loukes (8)	89
Heidi Muriel Snowden (8)	90
Connie Abdullah (8)	91
Clara Annie Martin (8)	92
Lily Isabella Page (8)	93
Ewan Johnston (9)	94
Zach Alexander Cosham (8)	95

The Edinburgh Academy

Charlotte Aoife Rose Clare Hurley (9)	96
Katie Dawson (10)	97
Andie Persaud (9)	98
Callum Legendre (10)	99
Erin Hood (10)	100
Zara Webb (9)	101
Anika Miedema (9)	102
Ben Finn (10)	103

THE STORIES

Splash

Splash! Andy got dropped into the blue sea of Crazyland. Andy lifted up a shell and put it in his pocket.
'Olopololoo!' sounded a voice from nearby, it was Multipul. She gasped and thought, *It's a human.* Then said, 'What are you doing here?'
Andy said, 'Who are you?'
She answered, 'I'm Multipul, who are you?'
And Andy said, 'I'm Andy.'
Multipul exclaimed, 'Let's go and defeat the land baddies!'
So they gathered a great army and defeated them all and won the first battle! They both went home. But will they live in mercy? No one knows...

Leen Nashed (9)
Bonaly Primary School

The Twins: Zelbar And Rablez

Zelbar and Rablez were monster twins. They didn't look like it. Zelbar was strong but Rablez was weak and small. I think he was jealous. They crash-landed yesterday on Earth. Rablez was talking about how to bomb the world. Zelbar heard! Just when Rablez was starting to put his plan into action, Zelbar lifted him up and threw him into a cellar!
'Hooray!' shouted everyone. 'Hooray! Hooray! Zelbar saved the day!'
But did he? Later, Zelbar was bringing some food but Rablez wasn't there. 'Oh no,' exclaimed Zelbar. 'Noooo!'
If something mysterious happens, check because it might be Rablez!

Isobel Morrice (9)
Bonaly Primary School

The Incident!

Ring, ring, ring went the bell at the end of the school day. Loyalty rushed out with her three best friends, Corney, Kitty and Smug, and they all went to Loyalty's house to go swimming.
'There's someone at the door,' trembled Corney.
'I'll get that,' said Loyalty.
Two hours later, Loyalty still was not back. Kitty, Corney and Smug were suspicious and they went to find her! They found Loyalty in a cave. Loyalty was kidnapped by the person who came to the door.
'You don't think that it was Rover, do you?' rumbled Kitty.
'It was,' sighed Loyalty.

Erica Louise Sibley (9)
Bonaly Primary School

Torrential Talonasaurus!

Here on Planet Anghtatexynga, it was Agnaday, and Zim-Zoom was going for his early run around his massive planet. Suddenly, he sprang too high and catapulted himself off his planet into outer space. He fell and fell, then... *bang!* Zim-Zoom faceplanted into sand. *Is this my planet?* thought Zim-Zoom. *No, it can't be because my planet has trees.* He had landed on the planet Blahboom. Then he heard a terrible rumbling and he saw his worst enemy, Talonasaurus. He gaped, and goggled, then Zim-Zoom sprinted. Then he leapt but he missed his planet! What would happen to Zim-Zoom next?

Calum Dall (9)
Bonaly Primary School

Flowjo Becomes Heartbroken

Flowjo lived in Maine. Her meadow was full of brightly coloured flowers and dewy grass.
One day, Flowjo thought, *there couldn't be anywhere better to live besides my wonderful meadow.* Then she happily lay her pretty head down and fell asleep. She had once thought enemies didn't exist but she was wrong... Flowjo had woken up, children were playing joyfully; joy is like music to Flowjo. So she rose up, breathed in flowers and out shot bright flowers for the children who thought she was being mean. So they threw stones at her! Flowjo was heartbroken but didn't show sadness...

Kaylie Coleman (9)
Bonaly Primary School

The Fourstrike

Long ago, lived the Fourstrike. The Fourstrike had a snake-like body and four fangs. It lived in the forest.
'Arghhhh!' Ben woke up screaming like mad! He checked his clock, it was twelve at night. *I can go to the forest*, he thought. Off he went.
He had just started, when *whoosh!* Out came the Fourstrike, it stopped, then the Fourstrike sprang up onto Ben's arm.
'He loves me,' Ben shouted.
But then, Ben noticed it was time to go home. When he got home, his mother was pleased to see him. He ran upstairs and jumped into bed.

Eilidh Chisholm (9)
Bonaly Primary School

Plapple Escape

After the battle, Pigeons versus Plapples, Shappa (a plapple) was forced to run. However, Quabble (a pigeon) went with her. Pigeons are four centimetres tall and have a horn that zaps lasers and wings to help them fly. They had to get away quick so Shappa jumped on Quabble's back and they flew away.
'Oh no!' whispered Shappa, 'I left evidence.'
Quabble used her long distance laser to blast the evidence. It was hard to find a suitable place to live because Quabble had thin skin and Shappa had furry skin but eventually they found a suitable place. Happy days!

Rachel Rose (9)
Bonaly Primary School

Kaboom

Shandy Sand Hand trudged along the hot sandy desert of Planet Plain. Suddenly, a giant sandstorm swooped across the desert, blowing everything in its path. Shandy quickly dug into the ground using his many hands. As he was burrowing himself, he found a hole. It was dark, but he used his laser eyes. There was a dark brown goo! He'd heard of it before, it was called 'mud'. Suddenly, a mole snuck up behind him!
'Ah, you're one of those sand monsters, there's no water that way,' he sneered.
It was a naughty mole... he dug into a lake...
Kaboom!

Rosie Forster (9)
Bonaly Primary School

Sugar Puff's Crazy Dream

Once upon a time, in Crazy Candy Sea, a Mercorn called Sugar Puff decided to throw a party. She invited all her friends, set up everything and got ready. Then all the guests arrived. The party was going great, until *boom! Crash!* Someone had crashed the party! Sugar Puff knew who it was! The Icy Moos! Sugar Puff's worst enemies. She was so mad! Worst of all, they took the cake. 'Noooooo!' cried Sugar Puff. Then she giggled, 'Wait a puff. That was just a dream.' And with a puff, she burst out laughing and said, 'I really am crazy!'

Lucy Meiklejohn (9)
Bonaly Primary School

The Attack Of The Aliens

'We're under attack!' yelled Mythical Magic.
Oh hello, meet Mythical Magic. He is normal like you, apart from his giant legs (he uses these to kick well), his sharks arms (he uses these to defeat enemies). Anyway, back to the story.
'We're under attack from aliens!' shouted the people of Edinburgh.
'Don't worry, I'll save us,' said Mythical Magic.
So he took on the aliens and one by one, the aliens fell. Now Mythical Magic is worldwide famous and on the front cover of every newspaper around the world!

Daniel William Leslie (9)
Bonaly Primary School

The Big Burny

Burny is a bad guy. He lives on the sun. His enemy is Bone Head and Burny tries to kill him. Burny's tricks and skills are scary, big, fly, fire, never die, shoot fire and can disappear. Burny finds Bone Head crushing the town. So Burny puts him into a net and burns his bum. Bone Head shouts so loud that every window smashes.
Finally, Bone Head tells Burny, 'Please stop, we can be friends and stop trying to defeat each other.'
So Burny says, 'OK, as long as we can defeat the Power Rangers.'
'OK,' Bone Head says.

Ben Sharman (9)
Bonaly Primary School

The Dragonfly Stealers

'Those pesky Dragon Stealers!' shouted Boogily Rex. Boogily Rex was one of the many creatures on Boogily Gagily, it's a jungle planet. Boogily Rex had four feet, scales on his body, a long tongue and six eyes. He could morph into anything. The Dragon Stealers had stolen their statue of Gagily Beelo, their founder. Boogily Rex was going to get it back, so he tracked through the most dangerous jungle of all. He managed to make it through and climbed up to the nest. He took the statue back down the mountain, trying not to get spotted. Rex headed off.

James Allen (10)
Bonaly Primary School

Jammy's Adventure

Jammy was leaving his home planet Zooolla to go to the shops. Suddenly, he realised that he was low on saucer fuel. He steered off course. After that, he crashed onto an unknown planet. It was dry on Jammy's feet, it felt as if it had a dreadful atmosphere. He suddenly saw his enemy, ZamZam, who glared at him like a lion. ZamZam strutted up to Jammy and punched him. Jammy stood like a brick wall. Jammy took things into his own hands and decided to 'boot' ZamZam off Planet Arooogaa like a football. Then, Jammy returned back home.

Jack Cook (10)
Bonaly Primary School

Battle Or Not?

Spud lives in a village called VIP. It gets attacked by giant spiders. Spud normally gets into trouble. They normally lose.
One day, they got attacked by giant spiders. They had lost half of their men but somehow Spud was still alive. He was hanging from a branch he had just set on fire.
Suddenly, the door slammed open and the tribe came in and said, 'We have won the battle, yes!' They'd never had a battle like this, but suddenly, there was a big thump on the door, had they won? Or was the battle still going? Uh-oh!

Emily McGillivray (9)
Bonaly Primary School

Stinky Mermaid Takes Over!

After Great got his new computer, he went online to see his friends. He met Hairy Dragon. He also met Shape-Shifter. Great met his worst enemy, Stinky Mermaid as well. Stinky Mermaid was on video chat and said, 'Mwahahaha! I will take over Pepereta and it will be mine! Mine!'
When Great heard that, he rushed outside and used his clever, fast flying skills to save the world. He saw Stinky Mermaid using her supersonic laser beams to burn a house. Great picked up a rock with his wand and threw it at her. He lived happily ever after.

Zohaib Jafar (9)
Bonaly Primary School

Marzoploit In Trouble

Firedash lives on Marzoploit. Lately, things have been going wrong because of Waterdash, a villain. Firedash can shoot fire and she can dash fast. Villain Waterdash was her enemy and she froze her. Firedash was stuck in a big ice cube. But one year, it was hot so she was free again.
One day, Marzoploit went dark. Firedash and Waterdash were scared, so they became acquaintances. They found out that it was Evilpaw, a villain. He was very mean, but they had got rid of one villain so at least they only had one left to defeat on Planet Marzoploit.

Lauren E Rhynas (9)
Bonaly Primary School

Mr Octopus

Mr Octopus lived deep underground in an old mineshaft. He was green and had four arms and legs. No one knew where he came from, or how he got there? All they knew was that he was not nice. Mr Octopus had no enemies but still didn't like anyone. But all that was about to change.
One morning, another monster came, bigger than him! The other monster scratched him. Mr Octopus was scared, so he scratched back! The other monster screamed and then five other monsters appeared behind him, bigger and stronger. Was this the end of Mr Octopus?

Alexander Dey (10)
Bonaly Primary School

The Cave Escape

Pettlefly was a monster with blue petals for protection and yellow skin as camouflage. She was on the beach when she accidentally stood on a rock. *Smash!* The rock broke and Pettlefly fell into a cave. There were two ninjas there. Just when she was about to fly out with her magic bracelet, the ninjas stole it and got away. All Pettlefly was left with, was a piece of rope. So she quickly made a ladder out of the rope, then climbed out. The ninjas also dropped her bracelet, so she got it back. But where had the ninjas gone?

Kirsty Elizabeth Arnot (9)
Bonaly Primary School

Niumond Island Trouble!

Niutop was sitting calmly on his beach bed singing upside down, the bed was more like a flattened toilet. He was wondering what to do when suddenly he fell with an unfortunate thump on the ground and weirdly, his arms fell off!
'Why is everything weird?' thundered Niutop. 'This must be the job of Red Squirrel. He is very sneaky!' Just then, from on top of him, cocoa beans were being tossed out of the loud waving tree. He thought it was Red Squirrel. 'The revenge is on Red Squirrel,' bellowed Niutop...

Angus Hunter (10)
Bonaly Primary School

The Creepy Adventure With Butch

'Hello, I'm Butch. My life's great. I have a year's supply of snow-cones and I live in an igloo. By the way, I am a yeti. Enough talking! Let's play some games. How about football?'
Butch got a ball, he got goals set up, but forgot the most important thing, he needed someone to play with him. His friend lived miles away. So, he set off. There were really high winds. He walked up the valley, and when he got to the top, he slid down the other side. He got to the house, rang the bell, but no answer...

Nell Hauxwell-Douglas (9)
Bonaly Primary School

The Adventures Of Koblob

Koblob slowly trudged down the hill of Nuclear Dimension. His red fur was sweaty. When he reached his spaceship, he leapt in and sped off to war. Just as he got there, the battle began. Koblob flew in and saw his evil older brother Noblob. Koblob shot his nuclear cannon at Noblob. It hit! It blew up all of Noblob's spaceship and Noblob himself. When Koblob returned to Nuclear Dimension, he was a hero in many monsters' eyes. He even got a medal from Mayor No-Eyes who had no eyes. Not one! But Koblob knew Noblob lived on.

Joseph Cebula (9)
Bonaly Primary School

The Bat And The Beast

One day, in a distant world, a huge volcano erupted all over Korok Planet Plains. It forced a bat-like creature called Elfbat, the last of his species, to an island in a huge cove that was very dangerous. On that island, he found a tiger-like species who hunts him everywhere. Elfbat was too tired to fly and had to hide.
That night, Elfbat fought the creature and got a lot of cuts, but it was a fair fight. Elfbat finally got the creature against a tree, but he did not hurt him. He actually helped him to survive...

Aidan Hughes (10)
Bonaly Primary School

The Laser Cyclops

In an ice cave, in Antarctica, a strange creature called Robert flew through. Then shortly after, a cyclops ran past, zapping Robert. Robert was a short, puffy thing with wings. Luckily, Robert got around a corner and escaped. Sadly when Robert got home, his home was destroyed. The story was that, a few years back, the cyclops came and now wreaks havoc. Robert decided to try to get the cyclops out. The plan was to try and tease the cyclops out and then make the spikes on the roof fall down and block it. Would it work?

Alexander Stott (10)
Bonaly Primary School

The Adventures Of Cupp Moo

Once, there was a land full of candy with a crazy creature called Cupp Moo. Everything about him was candy! He had an arch-enemy who lived in a volcano. So one day, Cupp Moo set off!
Two days later, he was finally there. And... there he was! Sitting in his throne was his enemy Cake Monster. 'I have been waiting for this day for a long time.'
The battle carried on for days, months, years! At the end, who knows what happened. That is the story of our hero Cupp Moo and the evil Cake Monster.

Leo Edge (9)
Bonaly Primary School

The Sun Disaster

Wiggle Diggly has one million eyes and his hands are so long, that they are more than a mile. He has one hundred hands and legs! Wiggle Diggly thought of how good being in the sun was. So one day, he went on a trip to the sun with his spaceship.
'Oh no! I forgot that I melt to fire. The sun is going to burn me.'
Meanwhile, 'Where am I?'
Wiggle Diggly was so confused where he was. But then he realised that he was on Wiggle Planet.
'Wow, I'm actually alive.'

Johny Pleki (9)
Bonaly Primary School

Through The Sky

Sky looked like a bat, but she was pink with blue eyes, horns, wings and feet. She was flying so fast, she got lost and landed on Earth. There were billions of birds, so she flew into a nest. By the way, Sky is really, really tiny! Suddenly, a golden eagle saw her. He chased her all the way to the hospital. Sky slipped through an air vent then went under a bed to get her breath back. Then she escaped through a different vent and flew as fast as she could, through the galaxy back to Planet Omn.

Anna Quin (9)
Bonaly Primary School

Crazy Creatures

There was a guy called Jeff who lived in Edinburgh. One day, he woke up on a secret testing laboratory in space. He escaped using an escape pod. When he got back home, he felt a bit different, so he went to look in the mirror. He realised that he was obsidian. He ran down the stairs, trying to be fast. When suddenly he was lightning quick! He then jumped out of his door and a cloud appeared below him. He was flying! He kept his superpowers to himself until super villains come to Earth.

Kealan O'Shea-Morrans (9)
Bonaly Primary School

The Runaway

Tulindu lived on the really hot planet of Bong and loved gymnastics. He was really big and fluffy and had two heads that could figure out two things at the same time. He was moving to Earth to go to boarding school, but was scared that he wouldn't get in. He decided to run away in case he didn't like it. When he ran away, he met his worst enemy, Elsie. But she had run away too. He realised that it was a bad idea to run away on the big planet of Bong and set off to Earth...

Anna Edwards (9)
Bonaly Primary School

Bimbil's New Home

Long ago, there lived an alien called Bimbil. He had green spots on his body and an eye on his head. Bimbil's skill was to turn invisible. He had no home, so he moved to a house on Planet Earth. Every day he would take something from the house and put it under the bed. Soon he had made a den. Bimbil had been able to avoid the boy who lived there by turning invisible. But, one day, the boy named Andrew saw him. He was so scared, he ran away and was never seen again.

Jemima Macaulay (9)
Bonaly Primary School

The Bloody Swamp

A monster called Sam lurks around the Bloody River. He will freeze your feet and take your eyes. He will shape-shift into someone you know. You don't know where he is, so you better watch out! He has two heads and ten fingers on each hand but only six toes with six legs. He lives in a cave and comes out at night, gets his eyes and gives you a fright! He can smell your eyes from miles away and come for you. Back at his cave, he eats your eyes one by one.

James Stark Millar (9)
Bonaly Primary School

Flash Superhero

Flash can run fast. He can fly. He has one eye, he's blue with green wings and yellow eyes. He lives on Cheese planet. He went to Super Superhero College with his enemy. Cheese Cheddar uses a cheese weapon to stop Flash and to eat the planet. But Flash manages to freeze Cheese Cheddar with his flashing eyes. Flash grabs him and flies to a nearby planet, a Peppy planet. But will Cheese Cheddar ever come back to Cheese planet?

Orlagh Belle Kennedy-Darke (9)
Bonaly Primary School

War Of Forever

Once, there was an alien and his name was Bob. He lived on Planet Jeff. His past was as bad as death. This is how he did his best to kill all the Bermys. Once most of the Bermys paid the price. Trade deals got broken and most of his race started to die out. Bob was now the leader. He went to war with the Bug Empire, only to get most of his race destroyed. Bob was very, very sad. The Bug Empire killed Bob and every tribe!

Magnus Johnston (10)
Bonaly Primary School

Nick And Leo's Crazy Creature Adventure

Daniel and Leo lived in Candyland with crazy creatures. They went to a very old cave and found a strange item called the Thana. Next, they went to defeat the one and only, Francis of Terror! Daniel and Leo struggled to fight him, but they forgot they had the Thana. Eventually, they defeated him once and for all. Finally, they got back home safe and sound with the Thana still with them.

Daniel Haxton-Locke (9)
Bonaly Primary School

Fluff Balls

'Ow!' said Kyutie as she was knocked into the sky.
'Hi, I'm Jumble Bumble,' said Jumble Bumble.
'Oh,' said Kyutie, 'I'm Kyutie. What are you doing here?'
'I'm on my way to fight crime!' replied Jumble Bumble.
'Can I come?' asked Kyutie.
'Yes, sure!' replied Jumble Bumble. 'Let's go.'
As they reached England, they approached Spyk MkSpikeyface. 'I've been waiting!' said SMSF.
'We know,' said JB.
They fought for hours. After the fight, which JB and Kyutie won, Kyutie and JB flew home. A group of people were begging to get their autographs. They were famous.

Evie Montgomery (9)
Bruntsfield Primary School

Tumble Bumble

While Tumble Bumble was flying, he suddenly banged into Cutie McBobbieface.
'Ouch!' said Cutie and Tumble Bumble.
'Where are you off to?' said Cutie.
'I am going to England to fight crime,' said Tumble Bumble.
'Can I go with you?' said Cutie.
'Sure!' said Tumble Bumble.
'Let's go fight crime,' said Cutie and Tumble Bumble.
A year later, they defeated Bobbie McBobbiepants by throwing him on the floor and bouncing on him like a bouncy castle. Two weeks later, they got a statue in their honour, it was of Cutie McBobbieface and Tumble Bumble.

Eilidh Broster (9)
Bruntsfield Primary School

What The Boom!

Boom Boom Bomb and Skelebones travelled to the forest by private jet. The forest was dark and wet. They heard little rustles now but they weren't scared.
Suddenly, the Kittycat Squad jumped out of the leaves. Boom Boom Bomb exploded on sight. Skelebones chucked Boom Boom Bomb at the Kittycat Squad but there were too many of them and they surrounded Boom Boom Bomb and Skelebones. The Kittycat Squad wrapped Boom Boom Bomb and Skelebones in yarn and took them to their leader, Congo Kitty. Boom Boom Bomb's family came to rescue them and they all exploded at once. *Bang!*

Bailey Geddes (10)
Bruntsfield Primary School

Salty And The Giant Squid

Salty was having a normal day, bathing in the Pacific. Suddenly, he felt bubbles down below. It was the squid. *Oh no*, thought Salty as he powered through the water using his super fins. He held his breath for ages and ages as the annoying red squid circled him.
'Where are you going?' said the squid laughing merrily.
'I'm bathing today,' said Salty scared.
'Well, we're looking for dinner...' they said.
Salty swam as fast as he ever swam before and finally got away. He spent the rest of his day playing with his friends in the nice, hot sun.

Mae Bailey (9)
Bruntsfield Primary School

The Seapora

The slimy Seapora planned to attack humans. He slid out of the water into Edinburgh and strangled 20,000 people. The humans were going to fight back. They made a ring of fire around the Seapora and made torches to frighten him. He was terrified. The humans captured him and put him in a cage but Seapora shape-shifted into crumbs. The guard did not realised that the crumbs were Seapora, so the guard brushed him out. *Humans are dumb*, the Seapora thought to himself. Suddenly, an elephant bounced Seapora to Neptune.
'Bye-bye,' the elephant called.
The humans felt smug.

Katie Tennet (10)
Bruntsfield Primary School

Run Away

Scarlett was running from Googly Eyes. It started to get sunny. 'Yay!' said Scarlett. She grew a tail and horns but Googly Eyes grew very tall. She ran to her spaceship. When she got in, she drove to a strange planet. When she got there, it began to rain and she became a mermaid. When she landed, three people saw her, they made friends. They were called Tom, Seren and Eilidh. They helped Scarlett hide from Googly Eyes.
'Can you help me get home without Googly Eyes knowing?'
'Of course,' said Tom.
'Your spaceship is there, you need to run!'

Erin Mahal (9)
Bruntsfield Primary School

The Safe Breaker

Briggan scrambled through the darkness with his little red chubby legs running wildly. Then he remembered where he was. He was in Ringo, Pluto's richest bank. Briggan turned a corner and saw a security guard. He used one of his abilities, making his eyes grow large. Tentatively, he approached the guard. The guard's eyes, all 23 of them, seemed oddly blank.
'Fall asleep!' commanded Briggan.
The guard collapsed. He rammed his jet-black horns in the lock. His horns melted into the shape of the key and the lock clicked open. He was in! He had broken into Ringo.

Edward Roberts (9)
Bruntsfield Primary School

The Shape-Shifter

There was a pencil on my desk. It wasn't there before - I hadn't touched it yet, but as I reached out to touch it, suddenly it changed into a ruler! What was this? It must be a shape-shifter.
'Fine, you got me,' said a voice.
'Who are you?' I asked.
The ruler turned into the shape of a boy.
'I was on your desk because I wanted a friend,' said the boy. 'Will you be my friend?'
'I guess so,' I said.
I was very happy that day. The day I made a shape-shifter friend. I'll cherish that day forever!

Robyn Sarah Lane (10)
Bruntsfield Primary School

The Adventures Of The Darkest Chicken

Once, there was a dragon-winged, poison-fanged, long-legged chicken called Bigwing.
One day, Bigwing waddled down to Bruntsfield Primary School. He decided to wait in the classroom for all of the pupils and teachers to come back inside. Then the bell rang and everybody came inside and Bigwing leapt at the teacher and killed it. Bigwing thought teachers were not important enough to be called he or she or Miss… or Mr… so instead he just referred to them as it! Next, he waited in the assembly hall. Then he went back home and watched TV with his family. Yay!

Tilly Jo Harkes (10)
Bruntsfield Primary School

The Canivourosapocaluk

It was a cold and lonely night and Canivourosapocaluk had just finished his supper. When he was going home, he saw something - a toilet! He fell in and suddenly, something came in. Before he could ask what was going on, the human sat on the toilet and did a large doodoo. He was honoured but before he could ask any questions, the human flushed the toilet and poor Canivourosapocaluk said, 'Arghhhh! I am tossing and turning like a fish, I am not amused.'
Then a frog came to him.
'Safe at last,' he giggled, 'I am now completely amused!'

Camille Renwick Wilson (9)
Bruntsfield Primary School

The Lurp

There was once a creature called The Lurp. He was very big and stinky, so no one liked him very much. He didn't mind. The only thing he liked was trees. One day, he was curled up in bed, when he heard some strange flopping noises outside his tree house. He looked out his window-hole and saw a terrifying, fire-eyed pancake! Although he was big, The Lurp wasn't very clever. He crawled over to greet the Lurp-eating pancake. Obviously, as soon as the pancake saw Lurp, she opened her flat, big mouth and swallowed him up! Apparently, he tasted terrible!

Ida Mackay (9)
Bruntsfield Primary School

Chakahara

Chakahara was in a classroom then he smelt a teacher's drink, he flew over to it. But this time the teacher saw him, he dove towards the drink but it moved. Chakahara kept trying to get the drink. Chakahara was furious, he charged at the teacher. The teacher dodged and whacked Chakahara. Chakahara whacked the teacher with his tail. The teacher had a broken leg and arm, nobody wanted to come back to the school. The kids built a statue of Chakahara. Chakahara went back home to Planet Zazzor. When he got back, Chakahara partied 'til the end of time.

Amelia Page (9)
Bruntsfield Primary School

The Unknown Creature

Deep down in the dark, spooky school basement lay the unknown creature. Many people tried to see this unknown creature but none succeeded, until one day when a little girl opened the squeaky door of the basement. She found a small puff of pink out of the corner of her eye before it disappeared into thin air. She went day after day, seeing more and more. However, on the last day the creature wasn't hidden. In fact, it was bouncing in the middle of the basement, standing out with its colourful, bright stripes. This creature is now known as Hidey.

Teema Siddiki (9)
Bruntsfield Primary School

Bowling Ball Bob

One day, Bob the pig was eating his food but someone had put in the wrong food. Suddenly, he turned into a gigantic bulging bubble. He started to walk but ended up knocking down everything in his way, like an angry charging elephant. He shot off like a speedy race car around the farm. Uh-oh! There was the farmer. *Crash!* He knocked the farmer down like a bowling pin. The power activated every time he ate. Sometimes it got a little annoying. Now he loved smashing things. Luckily, the power wore off after a week. It did… well hopefully.

Ailsa McGregor (9)
Bruntsfield Primary School

Gobbler And His Toothpaste Adventure

It was a normal Wednesday night and Gobbler was scuttling around the bathroom. He wore a little army helmet. It looked weird on him, with his eight legs and no arms. He was just a mouth on legs. He was on the hunt for toothpaste, his species survive on it. He was at the cupboard. *Creak, creak* the cupboard door opened. He lifted the heavy weight. He made his way back through the obstacles and saved his tribe. They all enjoyed the gigantic tube of toothpaste and all has been well since then, scuttling back and forth through the kitchen.

JJ Liggins (9)
Bruntsfield Primary School

Blurth

Weird Thingy had a thought that he would have a vacation. He told his parents he wanted to. He went off. In his spaceship, his biggle boggle juice spilt on a button. That button was very dangerous. He landed on a soft thing but it was white. He heard some things like, 'We're almost at the top of Mount Everest.'
He got scared so he slipped into a cave.
A boy came, he said, 'Hello. Let me teach you how to speak English.'
Eventually, he learnt English. His spaceship was fixed in time, he went home to his parents.

Ritika Sharma (9)
Bruntsfield Primary School

Spike

Spike was a small ball that had poisonous spikes all around him. When he was scared, he shot out his horrible spikes. His dream was never to be afraid of anything at all.
One normal day, Spike went to the funfair because he wanted to scare the children and rule over fun, but it never worked. While he was thinking about ruling over fun, a child spotted him. Spike was panicking. He closed his eyes hoping that the child would not touch him, but it wasn't a child. It was Dolly, Spike's best friend, so Spike wasn't scared.

Eva Jourdan (9)
Bruntsfield Primary School

The Legend Of The Supersonic Monster

Once, there was a world with a supersonic monster named Laser Some. His awesome world was called Rocktopia. There were lots of rocks there for it to shoot. Suddenly, an evil force attacked the planet Lucianos. The evil force was called Anti-Lucianos. To be precise, Planet Lucianos was not a planet, it was a demi-god planet. Anyway, Planet Lucianos was under attack. Laser Some went to the rescue. He punched, zapped and killed. Laser Some was a skilled fighter and had never lost a battle. Laser Some saved Planet Lucianos once again!

Elwyn Ichikawa-Bryant (9)
Bruntsfield Primary School

Bobzi

On Planet Boo, a little cute ball is on the candyfloss ground, looks like a normal ball, eh? It is sleeping. Her name is Bobzi. She is an ally to everyone and she has no enemies. Suddenly, the ground shakes and a creature touches Bobzi. 'Boo!'
Bobzi gets such a fright that she shoots glitter out of her mouth into the creature's face. Then he starts bouncing around. It turns out that he is a friend but it is too late, he has been knocked into The Other World. And that is the conclusion of the mini saga story.

Elektra Skye Robertson (9)
Bruntsfield Primary School

Mrs Crazy

One day, Mrs Crazy went to Mars then that day, one hour later, she turned into an alien.
A day later, she went to Mars again but that time she met a friend called Camosie and Camosie was the same as Mrs Crazy. Their first adventure was they punched a colossal hole in Mars, then they ran all around Mars one thousand times but the nine hundreth and ninety-ninth time, they met the alien council and the alien council said they could have a world record for running around Mars one thousand times. Then they went down in history.

Sophie McIntosh Burrows (9)
Bruntsfield Primary School

Doubless Found

One day, a vicious doubless, named for its double tails was in an abandoned mansion. He had just killed a lamb. After the meal was complete, he heard something like a bee in the sky. This was not good. This was a call of another doubless in distress. He had to help! Doubless went outside, unfolded his wings and soared through the sky. A few minutes later, he got there. The calling stopped. He saw a man with a dead doubless at his feet and a camera in hand. Then another rival doubless came, confronting ours. The man escaped...

Joe Jannetta (9)
Bruntsfield Primary School

Rainbow The Unicorn

Once, there was a pink unicorn called Rainbow and she was having a tea party with the Queen. She was disguised as Nicola Sturgeon and she started to shape-shift in front of the Queen's beady eyes. She pretended to be a sweet kind unicorn that could just shape-shift into different things and she presented the Queen with a present. She opened it and inside was a book... a book that ate people's heads off! Luckily, the guards caught the naughty unicorn and she was taken to prison.
A few years later, she escaped...

Eva Xin-Xin Stickland (9)
Bruntsfield Primary School

Fox Of Ice

In the dark cave in Scotland, there was a fox frozen in thick ice. When the ice broke, the fox opened its eyes and got ready for its fight. Icy was the fox's name. At the battle, she spread her wings and flew. She did her death echo as Fire and Thunder pinned her to the floor. As Fire looked in her eyes, Icy used her water blast at them. Fire and Thunder fell to the edge of the cliff, roaring for help. Icy helped them, then between Fire, Water and Thunder, magic formed around their bodies, peace was made.

Natalie Lesniowolska (9)
Bruntsfield Primary School

Breethasaur

The breethasaur was lonely and sad. It killed everything. In the future, the human race and the animal race. The only things that were still alive were lavasaurus. They were dinosaurs covered in lovely lava. It was angry with the breethasaur. It fought the breethasaur but it couldn't win no matter how much it tried. Eventually, it gave up. It surrendered! But the breethasaur didn't kill it. It felt something it had never felt before - love. Then it hugged the lavasaur and they became best friends forever.

Leo Cassidy (9)
Bruntsfield Primary School

A Little Visit To Earth

Chomp was in her land, Cloud Cookie Land, when she decided to teleport to Earth. She had never been to Earth before. She arrived in the middle of the night. She wandered around, while she was walking she saw a human. Chomp ducked into shadows.

It was the morning, Chomp saw humans coming out of their houses. She saw they had paper in their hands and ran over and snatched all the paper. The humans got mad that Chomp ate all the paper, she had started a war. Chomp won, they built a statue of her, she was very happy.

Iona Ward (10)
Bruntsfield Primary School

Candy War

One day, Candpanda was on a walk. People always stared at her. Maybe it was because of her candyfloss body and her panda head or maybe because everybody tried to eat her! Then she declared war. In her town, she was tiny compared to all the other candy and she wanted to be big. She puffed and puffed herself up until she was the size of a blown up balloon. Suddenly, her huge bubble body popped. She realised she could be big and strong and still be fine the way she was. Remember to always be yourself like Candpanda.

Amber Hutton (9)
Bruntsfield Primary School

Squishy And His Quest To Get Up

It was a beautiful day. The four suns illuminated the many glass skyscrapers of Gastropolis, capital city of Gastronius. Squishy was gazing out of his window when he saw a teacher handing out homework but that homework was no ordinary homework. It was the homework monster! The shock, the horror! Squishy tried to get up but he couldn't. He needed a plan.
Ten minutes later, Squishy still hadn't gotten up, Squishy sighed and gazed out of the window. 'Well,' he sighed, 'at least I tried.'

Percy Sutherland (9)
Bruntsfield Primary School

Mr Googly's Adventure

Mr Googly was telling jokes on the street with a big smile on his green face. He was having a great time giggling on the pavement. Lots of people liked Mr Googly, especially because he always rubbed his moustache.
One day, Mr Googly went onto the street but no one came to listen to his jokes, so he went to look around. He saw that a human was telling jokes too! He got so alarmed, he was shocked. He was very angry but he got calmed down by his friend. Instead of getting angry, he just told a joke.

Marta Della Sala (9)
Bruntsfield Primary School

The Tale Of The Moustache Monster

Once upon a time, the Moustache Monster looked in a mirror and saw a few hairs on his upper lip that looked suspiciously like a moustache. As soon as he and his four heads saw this, they rushed to the happy hairdressers. There, Jim the hairdresser cut the two hairs off his upper lip and gave him the mirror. The Moustache Monster noticed the remains of a hair and turned red with anger. He was proud of his hairlessness and he never went to a hairdresser again and that's why he hates hairdressers.

Connor MacKenzie (9)
Bruntsfield Primary School

Slant

There was once a monster who loved ice cream called Slant. He went to the ice cream parlour in Mexico City. Slant liked most of the ice creams there. Once, on the conveyer belt he went into a machine and was made into an ice cream. Slant ate all the ice creams and nearly exploded because they were so delicious. Soon Slant applied for a job as ice cream seller. Slant sold his ice cream to children on hot days. The children didn't mind his weird looks because they loved the ice creams he sold!

Max Milne (9)
Bruntsfield Primary School

Fasty The Fluffy

'Oh what a good holiday that was, but I still prefer the sun,' I exclaimed. I'm Fasty the Fluffy and I live on Mars. I saw something falling out of the sky. It was a drone with a camera, then I realised it was polluting. I flew up and ate the legs, they were slightly chewy. It fell to the ground. I flew down and ran towards it, breathing fire. It made the camera burn but the engine blew up. I added it to my collection of drones. I flew to the log cabin on the sun. It was super.

Sam Beattie (9)
Bruntsfield Primary School

Crackling Cracker

The crackling cracker is a vicious beast. For all you know, it could be the fire in your fireplace! It absorbs the heat from your fire. So now you know what could have made your fire cold.
One day, it went to a baker's at night. It saw a small fire. It wanted to make it bigger and that's exactly what it did! As it hurled towards the fire, it dived in. Suddenly, the fire burst up and caught the house. So kids now you know what made the Great Fire of London.

Alex Thomson (10)
Bruntsfield Primary School

The Odd Adventure At The Toy Shop

One peculiar day, the Devil-eyed Demon was in a toy shop in Edinburgh. He was pretending to be a toy. A tiny two-year-old with blonde hair and green eyes was just about to go up and hug him. Now bear in mind, this monster is 106 centimetres in height. As the little girl picked him up, he was furious and raging. This monster was red and orange with sharp, spiky teeth! He wouldn't dare kill a human. To him, a human was like a lion. He stormed out furiously and that was the last of him.

Athena Xantho Sintoris (9)
Bruntsfield Primary School

Flingcer Versus Fireake

Flingcer was moving his cat-like feet towards the fire jungle to meet his enemy.
'Hello,' said Fireake. Flingcer was ready to use his superpower to punch him and throw him. Fireake was ready to use his fiery breath. They spat, they pounced, they spewed fiery breath and threw each other. The fight was almost over. Fireake did not want to battle anymore, nor did Flingcer. They became best friends. Even though they do not see each other much they are still best friends.

Max Johnston (9)
Bruntsfield Primary School

The Return

Derelistec lived on Planet Der. One night, he flew to Earth at midnight to kill people. Whenever his family was hungry, he went to Earth and killed. He killed 121 people and flew back to Planet Der. They had a feast and had some spare.

The next day, all the people on Earth decided to go to Planet Der, so they got some weapons and flew on loads of rockets. When they arrived, they saw a huge castle. They went to the castle and Derelistec and his family flew up and burnt them all.

Muhammad Kashif (10)
Bruntsfield Primary School

The Fun Park Horror

One day, Fleur and Saturn went to Earth from Jupiter. They went to a festival and had a really fun time. They looked for an empty space to shape-shift into a ride. They found the perfect spot to have their new ride, they would get it started and they would bite people and dump them in a big bin. The owner of the place walked by and went on the new free and really cool ride. What he didn't know was that it was no ordinary ride, it was a painfully, scary, dark death ride...

Sophie Adams (9)
Bruntsfield Primary School

The Final Straw

Denvillious soared fast across the sky with his dog, Minkle, on his silky soft back with his eight horns on his head, big red wings and black cloak, he scared the world. It then happened! A fiery blaze filled the world. From space, the Earth was a fiery ball. Xeno was down below with all the humans of the world. Denvillious was shot out of the sky. He was in a net.
'We have had it with your tricks!' they shouted. 'We will kill you now!' And so they did!

Finlay Lawson (10)
Bruntsfield Primary School

The Tale Of Smelly McSlug Face

My name is Smelly McSlug Face and this is a story about me! I lived in Sam's garden and he was so cruel! So one day, I tried to escape. I took Sam's hat, to disguise myself. 24 hours passed... a girl picked me up and instead of keeping my name, she changed it to Sally! Why? It was so boring! She gave me makeovers, so I escaped again. I was getting used to this. I saw a new boy who picked me up and took me home. I was very excited but... No! He had a sister too!

Ava McComb (10)
Bruntsfield Primary School

Fluffy The Pink Pompom

Once, there was a monster called Fluffy the pink pompom and she could hypnotise everyone. Sometimes, her family members thought she was not good enough to be in the family, so one day she decided to go outside and hypnotise people. So she went to a restaurant called Yummy Junk Food. She went in and she sat on top of the table and started hypnotising people. She hypnotised everyone then left to go to another restaurant for dessert and she did everything all over again!

Saba Rashad (9)
Bruntsfield Primary School

Mischievous Mystery!

Once day, Mischievous Milly went to Snot Town. She went to the drooling bow shop, she bought a red shiny bow. After, she went to lots of other shops, she bought clothes and shoes, at last she was done. She was really hungry. She went to a really fancy restaurant. She ordered some macaroni and cheese and cheesy chips. When she ate the macaroni and cheese she grew wings and when she ate chips she grew more and more legs. She still felt peckish so she bought ice cream.

Zara Rahman (10)
Bruntsfield Primary School

Invy And The Gravity Twist

Once upon a time, on Mars, Invy was looking for her friends but she couldn't. That's the problem about being invisible. She jumped as high as she could, but she got stuck in the air! She shouted help as loud as she could but no one heard her (well, they probably did, but she was invisible so yeah!). Then she did her special once-in-a-lifetime trick and turned non-invisible whilst falling down to the ground and that's when she found her friends.

Rosie Kate Zisman (10)
Bruntsfield Primary School

Drake The Dream Catcher

Drake captured Eilidh's dream in his antenna, then flew off to Seren's house, only to find her having a nightmare. He then flew out of Seren's house and tried to find someone else to give Eilidh's dream to. Suddenly, Drake spotted Amelia having a lovely dream so he decided to give it to her. Drake swerved in through the window and placed his antenna on Amelia's head. He then goes to make one more switch before the sun rises.

Aisling Tierney (9)
Bruntsfield Primary School

Pongola

Pongola was yellow with red spots and had a big tail with his brain in it. He also had a special power but he didn't know about that until today, when Pongola was playing his normal old tricks on the humans. He felt like he could control the human and from then, he loved getting spotted. He soon had a whole army of crazy creatures and humans. He then had a great idea to take over the world and he succeeded and ruled the world.

Millie Orr (9)
Bruntsfield Primary School

Gooey Nightmare

'I seem to be sticky,' moaned Drizzelda, squelching through the mud. 'I am going to go to that cave for the night.' Just then, she saw something shiny. She walked nearer. Then, all of a sudden, she was on Mars! And who was that? No it couldn't be... it was Goggle Splat! *Psh, psh, splat!*
'Phew, you're stuck to a wall... but what?'
'Arghhhh!' she screamed.
'Wait what, I'm in my room, it was just a nightmare.'
Drizzelda walked downstairs. Her pet goo worm jumped up to her shoulder.
'Hey Gluey, get off,' laughed Drizzelda. 'I'm glad I'm home.'

Jess Mitchell (8)
George Watson's College Junior School

Zap!

In the corner of the school basement, lay the sneakiest of the scariest creatures. His name was Zig-Bob-Bizz, not such a scary name but when you see him, he just looks awkward. It was an ordinary day in Oakwood Primary. In classroom 4B, things were about to get a bit more interesting. Zig-Bob-Bizz snuck in like a shark lurking through water. With his laser eyes, he zapped the classroom 'til it looked like a rubbish tip. An ear-piercing scream came from the classroom. With his rockets, he zoomed away, leaving the children confused. What had just happened? Strange!

Sarah Kerr (8)
George Watson's College Junior School

The Big Bang My Style

Tazershell was whizzing around the factory like mad, opening and breaking into locked, cool doors. Then he carefully looked around, not seeing the head engineer behind him. After, he carefully crept into the boiler. When he noticed that there was nothing there, Tazershell tried to get out, but the head engineer had turned the boiler on and it was sucking all his amazing power. The boiler amazingly got over loaded and blew up the factory! Thankfully, Tazershell was all right. The head engineer got out of the factory and into the great countryside...

Oliver Bond (8)
George Watson's College Junior School

How Fused Got His Superpower

Once upon a time, there was a monster called Fused. He landed on Planet Mars. More than one million monsters were there. The digital DNA monster was excited. He was first to fight. He had trained for many years. In fact, his opponent was his rival, Sobek the Egyptian god. He was really strong, so Fused got past his maximum power level without noticing. He released his superpower then drained Sobek's energy power. Sobek was so weak that he collapsed on the floor. The space police sent Fused to space jail for one year, eight months and fourteen days.

Noah Lucatelli (9)
George Watson's College Junior School

The Adventure Of Blobmcblob

One day, Blobmcblob was walking through a strange tunnel and walked into a strange world. There was no blobs or green stuff or blobs of green anywhere to be seen for miles around. All there was, was an icy coat and fog. Even ten metre mountains couldn't be seen in all this fog. Suddenly, a noise could be heard. It was a terrible noise, a mix between a screech and a yowl. It sounded like this, *scowl! What could it be?* Blobmcblob thought. It came closer and closer until he could see it clearly. It was a griffin... uh-oh!

Lucy Dunbar (8)
George Watson's College Junior School

Booger Meets Snot Face!

Crazy Booger Ball was flying through Snotville Town. Suddenly, he heard a squelch. Was it an enemy or friend? It was his arch-enemy Snotface! Booger turned invisible. Using his long tentacled eyes, he took aim and fired! Snotface was blinded by green slimy boogers. He let out a piercing roar. Booger used his googly eyes to hunt out Snotface's spaceship. Like a meteor, he zoomed through the air. Stealing the spaceship was his only way home to Planet Booger. He pressed the big green button marked *go* and blasted off for home.

Louis Ferguson (8)
George Watson's College Junior School

Untitled

Once, there was a tiny mental alien called Mental, zooming through the sky doing swoops and loops. Then his engine began to run out of fuel and crashed in the middle of the Indian Ocean. He transformed himself into a fish but at the same time, a big net caught him and poor Mental got trapped inside. Mental wriggled, ran and swam but it was no use. When he got to Earth, the crazy alien ran. An evil king saw him. He met a girl, her hair was lovely and long. Together they defeated the evil king and made peace.

Aditi Patwari (8)
George Watson's College Junior School

Gobodor Finds His Legs

Gobodor the Monster had lived 70,000,000 years without his legs, but today he decided he wanted them back! His legs had been ripped off by a pug and the pug had thrown them away. His dad, Gobblemack, had made him some hoverboard legs instead. But now Gobodor wanted real legs because he was jealous of people who had legs. But when Gobodor lost his legs, he was fine but now he was not. He went back to Earth and found his legs in a bin, he went back home. When he arrived, he squeezed his legs back on happily.

Stephen Carlos O'Neill (9)
George Watson's College Junior School

The Adventures Of Mega Oink

Mega Oink let out an almighty pig sound. Everyone in the world heard it. Mega Oink was furious! The Butcher had pignapped his best friend from Oink Planet called Carl. He was so angry he rode on the pig-mobile all the way to the super evil Butcher's kitchen. He tried to find him but the Butcher wasn't there because he was at the farm killing some more pigs to eat them for his tea. Mega Oink could not let this happen, so he started to fight him, then he bit his hand off and then the butcher died.

Finlay Joseph Riley-McLean (9)
George Watson's College Junior School

Zoozo's Strange Adventure

Zoozo was playing in the park in Pluto. Then suddenly, he was playing in a strange place. There was no monsters like him with fire eyes. Then there were weird things walking about. Zoozo was rolling about in the strange place. After, he was being attacked by giant eagles, Zoozo was scared but then he was confident. He fought the giant eagles. He killed all the eagles. Then Zoozo began to sing. The weird things were looking at him and they started to dance. Zoozo suddenly went back home to Pluto.

Jawan Fayez Fagiha (9)
George Watson's College Junior School

The Trickster

Sticky is a monster with seven eyes and can see more than four miles. He lives in the school bin, and tries to trick children by using his superpowers to shape-shift. He has sticky pads on his feet. He first tried to trick someone when he was three. It was quite good actually. I'll tell you what happened. He turned himself into a lovely, bright yellow and black striped pencil that any boy or girl would want to use. But when the girl used it, the pencil wrote in ink. The little girl was devastated.

Jasmine Mitchell (8)
George Watson's College Junior School

The End Of Humankind

Drama Queen Mermaid was being a drama queen. She heard the humans were coming into the inner core of the Earth. She screeched, 'I live here, I am not letting the humans take my land!' She jumped into the water at the moon pool and she turned into a mermaid, when she touched water. She used her fangs and drained the life out of her enemies. She was raging mad. She went to the surface of the Earth and started draining life out of everyone. Everyone was petrified, the ground started to shake...

Enam Evong (8)
George Watson's College Junior School

The Fire Adventure

One blazing hot day, in Volcano Land, King Kane the Beast was so bored at the palace. He thought of doing the most fun game in the land. He popped up on Earth. He was in Scotland. He saw a sign saying: *School* and went into Class II. In Class II, he sipped all the water bottles and turned them into lava. He found himself back in Volcano Land. He thought of having a lava bath in his volcano. He put his six hands up and slid down, the floor became burning hot lava, it was hot!

Aaron Loukes (8)
George Watson's College Junior School

Zoom Zoom's Sad Story

This is Zoom Zoom. He lives on Earth. Every once in a while, he visits an active volcano that is very dangerous.
One day, he went to scare a few people, but everyone vanished so he ran up to the volcano, but Zoom Zoom lost his balance and fell in. He couldn't burn but it still really hurt. He climbed out shaking, then he dived into some water and never set foot on land again. There was still some dried up lava on Zoom Zoom's head and it looked like he had cat ears.

Heidi Muriel Snowden (8)
George Watson's College Junior School

£10,000 Is Stolen From Slug Slumo Guy

One day, Slug Slumo Guy went to the theme park. He went on the Ghostbuster ride. There were curvy curves, terrifying drops and a crazy spin ride over a canyon with a rough river, but it was just an illusion. Slug Slumo Guy had lost his sixth baby eye. So he bought a packet of pens to draw them on. He was so fed up of using them that he stole ten thousand pounds. But then in the corner of his eye, he found a sack. He had found his six eyeballs in it. Slug Slumo Guy was so happy.

Connie Abdullah (8)
George Watson's College Junior School

Middle-Down-Town And The Kick Of Doom

Hi, I'm Middle-Down-Town. I have a secret button which makes me kick with my very long leg. We are going on an adventure. Let's go on the adventure and see if I need to press it or not. We are going to the forest.
Finally, we are here... but what is that whizzing around me? I am going to have to press the button, so I do. Suddenly, my long leg swings out and I hit the snake. Once I do that, I run home and I'm safe and sound there.

Clara Annie Martin (8)
George Watson's College Junior School

My Crazy Creature Saga

Flying Felicity was a harmless creature that was furry, pretty and brilliant at drawing and flying. Far, far away, on a planet called Mars, a creature called Flying Felicity strode out of a gigantic house. She saw her enemy, Bob Blader, was killing everybody! She flew up in the sky and used her wings to bring the people alive again and her enemy flew away in the sky. Then a policeman said, 'Well done, Flying Felicity! You are a hero.'

Lily Isabella Page (8)
George Watson's College Junior School

Blopin Hates Potholes

Blopin is walking along a road and he gets stuck in the pothole. His feet are too flat so he just slips back in. But his big smile is so big that a crane comes and helps him. Then Blopin can get on with his normal day. But as he keeps on walking, he gets very hungry and there are no shops. Then, over there in the distance he sees some. Blopin walks all the way there and, goes into a shop, gets food and comes out happy and full.

Ewan Johnston (9)
George Watson's College Junior School

Boogle!

There was once an alien called Boogle and he lived on Boogle Planet.
One morning, Boogle was having breakfast. After breakfast, he went outside but then the doodles came along and stole all the sweets that Boogle had taken out. Did I tell you about that? So Boogle pushed the doodles off the planet and was very happy.

Zach Alexander Cosham (8)
George Watson's College Junior School

The Eruption Of Kamakou

One day, Laser-Canick was slithering about scarily looking around a volcano when suddenly, *boom!* There was huge eruption from volcano Kamakou.

A few hours later, some miners came to the volcano to get some cool minerals. Although what they didn't know was that, Laser-Canick was lurking about. Laser-Canick was getting closer and closer when... *Arghhhh!* Laser-Canick pounced up on the miners. They all ran away never to go back to Kamakou again. So watch out, whenever you go out to Arthur's Seat or something, if you see a big, snake-like, fanged, sticky, spotty, laser-eyed creature... Run!

Charlotte Aoife Rose Clare Hurley (9)
The Edinburgh Academy

The Adventures Of Pastanimal

Pastanimal and Quinaosaurus were enemies. Pastanimal was a suave, smooth character whom everybody loved. Quinaosaurus was a newcomer to town, whom nobody liked.
One day, Quinaosaurus decided to take his revenge by capturing Pastanimal's daughter, Penne. He locked her in a room. What Quinaosaurus had forgotten, was that Pastanimal was able to make his body go soft and slippery. Pastanimal slid under the door of the hiding place in order to save his beloved daughter. Just when he thought he'd won the day, Quinaosaurus appeared. He had grown hugely in size and power. He confronted Pastanimal. How will they escape?

Katie Dawson (10)
The Edinburgh Academy

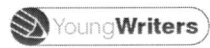

Oscar The Alien Visits The Dentist

Oscar's an alien monster who is very scared of humans. He also suffers from painful toothache. One day, the pain became so unbearable, that he couldn't take it anymore. Oscar needed help! Shaking and trembling as he walked the crowded city streets, he eventually found a dentist surgery with a sign saying: *Humans and Aliens Welcome*. Oscar found the courage to walk in. The kind dentist checked his teeth and found the problem, it was just a cavity. The dentist mended Oscar's tooth and rewarded him with a shiny sticker. Oscar was thrilled and was no longer afraid of humans.

Andie Persaud (9)
The Edinburgh Academy

Chumunga Hunt

The ferocious Ekarma crashes through the dense forest looking for a Kongbagon to eat. Eventually, it finds a Kongbagon but it's too late. A pack of Chumunga are already there! It starts to scare them off. First, it waves its tentacles around in a threatening way, but the Chumunga don't go. Then it unleashes a big roar and charges recklessly into the group of Chumunga. They scatter but instead of attacking the Kongbagon, they attack Ekarma! After a long battle, the Ekarma wins but during the battle, the Kongbagon leave. With no choice, Ekarma has to resume the hunt.

Callum Legendre (10)
The Edinburgh Academy

Your Teacher's Left Shoe

All teachers have a left shoe but your teacher is different. Your teacher's shoe is fluffy, it has an antenna, laser-beamed eyes and stuff like that. However, it has an enemy, your teacher's right shoe. Just like the left shoe, it has a habit of being favoured which, when it's not, it becomes very annoyed! Your teacher's left or right shoe aren't very nice. They both like making your teacher go where they want. That is why your teacher walks 'not very' straight sometimes. So the next time you see your teacher's feet, make sure to just check them!

Erin Hood (10)
The Edinburgh Academy

Fursocka Vs Mum

Mum was doing the laundry when she heard a noise. 'What was that?' she asked herself. She picked up the sock next to her and put all the socks into a basket. Out of nowhere, the socks formed into a creature. This creature was sort of cute. Legend had it, this creature was scared of everything. The creature was called Fursocka. Fursocka sneaked behind Mum to thank her for making him but when she turned around, he turned invisible. 'What is that smell?' she asked herself. Fursocka stunk like the smelliest cheese ever! People say he will leave socks everywhere.

Zara Webb (9)
The Edinburgh Academy

A Mischievous Creature And A Lethargic Librarian

It's not every day you catch a glimpse of a hairy hand reaching for a book from the shadows in the library. If you do, it's probably the Emeek, an insolent bookworm with a peculiar habit of changing colour depending on its mood. Despite its book addiction, its worst fear is the ominous librarian lurking around, waiting for furry intruders. When startled, it becomes invisible and when happy, enjoying a book, it shifts to a warm yellow. It turns blue when it's sad and when it's angry, fiery red and it blows up like a balloon to twice its size!

Anika Miedema (9)
The Edinburgh Academy

The Story Of Squiron

Once, in the deepest, darkest spot at the bottom of the fish tank, lived Squiron.
One watery day, he was rudely disturbed by the goldfish. The goldfish started to bully Squiron. He blew big, smelly bubbles at his face. Squiron was brave and pushed the goldfish against the wall of the tank. The goldfish hit the wall so hard he knocked a small toy trident off its shelf. The Squiron swam over to where the trident was, picked it up and that was that. Soon the Squiron guarded the fish tank from bullies. The Squiron lived happily ever after.

Ben Finn (10)
The Edinburgh Academy

Cranzie's Crazy Life

Cranzie slithered along drearily, he was the last of his kind and was determined to stay safe. Suddenly, Cranzie heard a Zantie bird, his sworn enemy. Cranzie knew the Zantie bird could grow like him and Cranzie could not fight it. It was too dangerous. The Zantie bird was closing in, he could either take his chances and take it on or run! Cranzie chose to run and slowly slithered away. He realised he could not go that fast and stopped. The Zantie flew over him. Cranzie slithered into his small hole and burrowed further into the hole.

Brodie Lindsay (10)
The Edinburgh Academy

My Dog Turns Evil

My dog may seem extremely cute, but there's more to him than meets the eye. Recently, he escaped my house, which is in Edinburgh and headed south for London! It's a miracle that he survived, running across the motorway at 100 miles per hour! Unfortunately, he made it to the Houses of Parliament and Theresa May wasn't pleased to see an evil dog standing in her office! She narrowly escaped the attack, and the Queen came to see what was going on. I reached London an hour later, and I was put in prison for no reason at all.

Ralph William Kelly (9)
The Edinburgh Academy

Untitled

I am Grescogian, and my spaceship can take me everywhere very fast. It is invisible and I enjoy seeing new planets and observing other creatures. This green, sunny planet is different. It's beautiful, but during the day, the flowers make me sneeze and my eyes pop out without warning. At night-time, these black-winged creatures attack me. I cannot find peace or rest like I do on my home planet but I am fascinated by it and want to explore more. The sun is not as hot like home so I have to wear a coat for extra warmth.

Ioannis Tsirikos (10)
The Edinburgh Academy

The Dream Devil

Once, there was an evil cat called The Dream Devil. He had fangs, horns, big red wings and his weapon was a huge pitchfork which always had lightning sparkling around it. The Dream Devil hid under pillows at night. He waited until children put their heads on their pillow and then, when they fell asleep, he struck them on their head and they got nightmares.

One day, he got spotted by a person so he ran away. So before you go to bed, check under your pillow to make sure The Dream Devil has not returned to you.

Lily Phanos (9)
The Edinburgh Academy

Dobob And The Great Escape

Dobob was a very naughty creature. He lived in dark places and ate bananas.
One day, he was in his cave when all the creatures of the world came and tried to get into his cave. But, they were too big. Dobob rolled into a ball and started to grab all his things. He then bounced out of his cave and on all the creatures' heads while they tried to catch him. When Dobob was hidden, he was relieved that he didn't get caught and he still heard all the creatures searching for him. Then he ate a big banana!

Alexander Millar (10)
The Edinburgh Academy

The Goofy Chase

Once, there was an alien named Goofy. He lived in Goofland.
One day, he decided to go to Earth, so he went. When he got there, he realised that the aliens there didn't like him so they chased him. To Goofy this was a strange planet. After being chased for a long time, Goofy found a secret hut in the woods. It was just the right size so he crept in. Goofy stayed there for four hours then started to feel hungry. He found berries close to his hut. He saw a ship from home. Then he got a lift!

Arianna Coli (9)
The Edinburgh Academy

The Cookie Jar

Once, there was a cookie jar. His name was Chocolate Cookie Jar. He lived in a house, but he was fed up of people eating his cookies so he decided to run away. He made a plan, he got a cellphone from his friend Goofy. He would go through the cat flap in the dead of the night and run away. He was very quiet not to wake up the fat cat. It was a long journey but he made it. Now his cookies were safe.

Zac Lawson (10)
The Edinburgh Academy

Est.1991

YOUNG WRITERS INFORMATION

We hope you have enjoyed reading this book – and that you will continue to in the coming years.

If you're a young writer who enjoys reading and creative writing, or the parent of an enthusiastic poet or story writer, do visit our website www.youngwriters.co.uk. Here you will find free competitions, workshops and games, as well as recommended reads, a poetry glossary and our blog.

If you would like to order further copies of this book, or any of our other titles, then please give us a call or visit www.youngwriters.co.uk.

Young Writers
Remus House
Coltsfoot Drive
Peterborough
PE2 9BF
(01733) 890066
info@youngwriters.co.uk